# Contents

# Being Me, *Loving You*

## A Practical Guide to Extraordinary Relationships

*A Nonviolent Communication™
presentation and workshop transcription by*

## Marshall B. Rosenberg, Ph.D.

*PuddleDancer*
PRESS

2240 Encinitas Blvd., Ste. D-911, Encinitas, CA 92024
email@PuddleDancer.com • www.PuddleDancer.com

*For additional information:*
Center for Nonviolent Communication
5600-A San Francisco Rd., NE, Albuquerque, NM 87109
Ph: 505-244-4041 • Fax: 505-247-0414 • Email: cnvc@cnvc.org • Website: www.cnvc.org

Being Me, Loving You
A Practical Guide to Extraordinary Relationships

© 2005 PuddleDancer Press
A PuddleDancer Press Book

PuddleDancer Press, Permissions Dept.
2240 Encinitas Blvd., Ste D-911, Encinitas, CA 92024
Tel: 1-858-759-6963  Fax: 1-858-759-6967
www.NonviolentCommunication.com  email@PuddleDancer.com

Ordering Information
Please contact Independent Publishers Group,
Tel: 312-337-0747; Fax: 312-337-5985; Email: frontdesk@ipgbook.com
or visit www.IPGbook.com for other contact information and details
about ordering online

Author: Marshall B. Rosenberg, Ph.D.
Editor: Graham Van Dixhorn, Write to Your Market, Inc.,
        www.writetoyourmarket.com
Cover and Interior Design: Lightbourne, Inc., www.lightbourne.com
Cover Photograph: www.gettyimages.com

Manufactured in the United States of America

1st Printing, May 2005

10  9  8  7  6  5

ISBN: 978-1-892005-16-8

# Being Me, *Loving You*

## A Q&A Session With Marshall B. Rosenberg, Ph.D.

The following are excerpts from workshops and media interviews given by Marshall Rosenberg on the subject of intimacy and close, personal relationships. Through role-playing and discussion, Marshall touches on most of the key aspects of applying Nonviolent Communication (NVC) to create loving relationships with our partners, spouses, and family, while maintaining our personal integrity and values.

## Introduction

So guess what happened today? I'm doing this relationship workshop in the evening, and I had a crisis at seven o'clock this morning. My wife called and asked me one of those questions that you just hate to have in a relationship at any time of the day, but especially at seven in the morning when you don't have your lawyer. What did she ask at seven o'clock in the morning? "Did I wake you up?" That question wasn't the hard one. She says, "I have a very important question: Am I attractive?" [Laughter] I hate those questions. That's like the time I came home after being on the road quite awhile and she asked me, "Can you see anything different in the house?" I looked and I looked: "No." She had painted the whole house! [Laughter]

I knew that question this morning was the kind that comes up in relationships. "Am I attractive?" Of course, as an NVC-speaking person, I could get out of that by claiming that it's not an NVC question, because we know that nobody "is" anything. Nobody is right, wrong, attractive, or unattractive. But I knew she wouldn't settle for any of that stuff, so I said, "You want to know if you're attractive?" She said, "Yes." "Sometimes yes, sometimes no; can I go back to bed?" [Laughter] She liked that, thank goodness, thank goodness! In one of my favorite books, *How to Make Yourself Miserable*, by Dan Greenberg, you see this dialog:

"Do you love me? Now, this is very important to me. Think it over: Do you love me?"

"Yes."

"Please, this is very important; give it very serious consideration: Do you love me?"

(Period of silence) "Yes."

"Then why did you hesitate?" [Laughter]

People can change how they think and communicate. They can treat themselves with much more respect, and they can learn from their limitations without hating themselves. We teach people how to do this. We show people a process that can help them connect with the people they're closest to in a way that can allow them to enjoy deeper intimacy, to give to one another with more enjoyment, and to not get caught up in doing things out of duty, obligation, guilt, shame, and the other things that destroy intimate relationships. We show people how to enjoy working cooperatively in a working community. We show them how to transform domination structures, hierarchal structures into working communities in which people share a vision of how they can contribute to life. And we're thrilled with how many people all over the world have great energy for making this happen.

## A Typical Conflict

Participant: Marshall, what do you think is the major conflict, the major issue between men and women?

Marshall: Well, I hear a lot of this in my work. Women come up to me regularly and say, "Marshall, I wouldn't want you to get the wrong idea. I have a very wonderful husband." And then, of course, I know the word "but" is coming. "But I never know how he's feeling." Men throughout the planet—and there are exceptions to this—come from the John Wayne school of expressing emotions, the Clint Eastwood, the Rambo school, where you kind of grunt. And instead of saying clearly what's going on inside of you, you label people as John Wayne would when he walked into a tavern in the movies. He never, even if there were guns trained on him, said, "I'm scared." He might have been out in the desert for six months, but he never said, "I'm lonely." But how did John communicate? John communicated by labeling people. It's a simple classification system. They were either a good guy—buy them a drink—or a bad guy—kill them.

With that way of communicating, which was how I was trained to communicate basically, you don't learn how to get in touch with your own emotions. If you're being trained to be a warrior, you want to keep your feelings out of your consciousness. Well, to be married to a warrior is not a very rich experience for a woman who may have been playing dolls while the men were out playing war. She wants intimacy, but the man doesn't have a vocabulary that makes it easy to do that.

On the other hand women are not taught to be very clear about their needs. They've been taught for several centuries to deny their own needs and take care of others. So, they often depend on the man for leadership and expect him to kind of guess what she needs and wants and to fulfill that, to take care of that. So I see these issues regularly, but as I say, there are certainly a lot of individual differences.

Participant: Let's do a role-play, the kind of thing that happens between men and women. Can you set it up? I mean, you know what they fight about the most.

Marshall: Well, one of the most frequent ones is the woman saying to the man: "I don't feel the connection with you that I would like. I really want to feel more an emotional connection with you. And how do you feel when I say that?" And the man says, "Huh?"

Participant: Well, yeah, let me play the man. [beginning the role-play] Well what do you want? What do you want me to do?

Marshall: Well, like right now, instead of asking me that question, I would like to know what you're feeling. Like, are you hurt by what I said? Are you angry? Are you scared?

Participant: I don't know.

Marshall: Yeah, and this is what I mean. When you don't know what you're feeling it's very hard for me to feel safe and trusting.

Participant: Well, I feel like you're . . . I feel like you're criticizing me.

Marshall: So, you're feeling kind of hurt and you want me to respect you and to appreciate what you offer in our relationship.

Participant: Well, yeah.

Marshall: And see, I would've liked for you to have said that. I would've liked to have heard you say I'm hurt, I'd like some appreciation. But notice you didn't say that. You said, "You're criticizing me." You required me to have to take a deep breath and not get caught up in that and not hear a judgment in what you say, and instead to try to hear what you're feeling and what you might need. I'd like not to work so hard at that. I'd really appreciate it if you could just tell me what's going on inside you.

Participant: Well, I don't know what's going on inside of me, most of the time. What do you want from me?

Marshall: Well, first I just am glad we're having this conversation now. I want you to know that I hope I can stay aware of how confusing it is to give me what I want. I'm trying to become conscious that it is such a new thing for you and I want to be patient. But, I would like to hear what's going on in you.

Participant: Well, right now, I guess I'm just glad that you're telling me what you need.

Marshall: So, that's a very typical kind of interaction that goes on. The man, he very often hears demands coming from the woman.

# On the Subject of Marriage

Marshall: You may have heard me say that it is harder to relate within a marriage than outside because of all the crazy things we are taught as to what "marriage" means. I find I enjoy the person I'm living with much more if I don't think of her as "my wife," because in the culture I grew up in, when someone says "my wife," they start to think of her as some kind of property.

NVC is a language that makes it possible for us to connect with one another in a way that enables us to give to each other from the heart. That means with your partner, you don't do things because of titles that imply you are "supposed to," "should," "ought to," or "must." You don't give out of guilt, shame, unconsciousness, fear, obligation, duty. It is my belief that whenever we do anything for one another out of that kind of energy, everybody loses. When we receive something given out of that kind of energy, we know we are going to have to pay for it because it was done at the other person's expense. I'm interested in a process in which we give to each other from the heart.

How do we learn to give from the heart in such a way that giving feels like receiving? When things are being done in a human way, I don't think you can tell the giver from the receiver. It's only when we interact with one another in what I call a judging, or judgmental, manner, that giving isn't much fun.

# Learning Through Four Questions

Let me suggest that you write some things down. I'm going to ask you four questions. If you are married or partnered, then pretend that you'll be speaking with your partner or spouse. If you want to focus on some other relationship, pick someone you're close to, perhaps a good friend. Now as your NVC partner, I'm going to ask you the four questions that deeply interest NVC-speaking people around all relationships, but particularly intimate ones. Please write down your answer to each of these four questions as though you were asked by this other person. Reader: We invite you to do this on your own on a separate sheet of paper.

The first question:

Would you tell me one thing that I do as your partner or friend that makes life less than wonderful for you?

You see, as an NVC-er I don't want to take any action or say anything that doesn't enrich your life. So it would be a great service if, anytime I do something that isn't enriching your life, you bring that to my attention. Could you think of one thing that I do—or don't do—that makes life less than wonderful for you? Write down one thing.

Now the second question. As an NVC-speaking person, not only do I want to know what I do that makes life less than wonderful for you, it's also important for me to be able to connect with your feelings moment by moment. To be able to play the game of giving to one another from our hearts, your feelings are critical and I need to be aware of them. It's stimulating when we can be in touch with one another's feelings. My second question then:

When I do what I do, how do you feel?

Write down how you feel.

Let's move to the third question. As an NVC-speaking person, I realize that how we feel is a result of what our needs are and what is happening to our needs. When our needs are getting fulfilled, then we have feelings that fall under the heading of "pleasurable feelings," like happy, satisfied, joyful, blissful, content . . . and when our needs are not being satisfied, we have the kind of feelings that you just wrote down. So this is question three:

What needs of yours are not getting met?

I'd like you to tell me why you feel as you do in terms of your needs: "I feel as I do because I would have liked _____ (or because I was wanting, wishing, or hoping for _____.)" Write down what you need in this format.

Now the NVC-er is excited because he wants to get on to this next question, which is the center of life for all NVC-speaking people. I can't wait to hear the answer to this. Everybody ready for the big NVC question?

I am aware that I am doing something that is not enriching your life and that you have certain feelings about that. You've told me what needs of yours are not getting fulfilled. Now, please tell me what I can do to make your most wonderful dreams come true. That is what NVC is all about:

What can we do to enrich one another's lives?

NVC is about clearly communicating those four things to other people at any given moment. Of course, the situation is not always about our needs getting met. We also say "thank you" in NVC and tell people how they have truly enriched our lives by telling them the first three things. We tell them (1) what they've done to enrich us, (2) what our feelings are, and (3) what needs of ours have been fulfilled by their actions. I believe that, as human beings, there are only two things that we are basically saying: "please" and "thank you." The language of NVC is set up to make our "please" and "thank you" very clear so that people do not hear anything that gets in the way of our giving to one another from the heart.

## Criticism

There are primarily two forms of communication that make giving from the heart almost impossible for people. The first is anything that sounds to them like a criticism. If you have expressed the four things that you have written in NVC, there would be no words written there that can be heard by the other person as a criticism of them. As you see, the only time you are talking about them is in the first part where you mention their behavior. You are not criticizing them for the behavior; you are just calling that behavior to their attention. The other three parts are all about you: your feelings, your unmet needs, and your requests. If there are any words in there that can easily be heard by the other person as a criticism, then my guess is that you've mixed a bit of judgment into those four ingredients.

By "criticism," I mean attack, judgment, blame, diagnosis, or anything that analyzes people from the head. If your answers are in NVC, there will hopefully be no words that are easy to pick up as criticism. However, if the other person has these ears [Marshall puts on a pair of judging ears], they could hear criticism no matter what you say. Tonight we'll learn how to clean up such a mess if it happens. We want to be able to speak NVC to anybody.

## Coercion

The second block to our ability to give from the heart is any hint of coercion. As an NVC-er, you want to be able to present those four things you wrote down such that the other person receives them as a gift, an opportunity to give, not as a demand or order. There is no criticism or coercion in the NVC language. When we tell others what we want, we do so in a way that communicates to them, "Please do this only if you can do so willingly. Please never do anything for me at your expense. Never do anything for me where there is the least bit of fear, guilt, shame, resentment, or resignation behind your motives. Otherwise we'll both suffer. Please honor my request only if it comes from your heart, where it is a gift to yourself to give to me." Only when neither person feels like they're losing, giving in or giving up, do both people benefit from the action.

## Receiving From the Heart

There are two main parts to NVC: the first is the ability to say those four things and get them across to the other person without the other person hearing criticism or demand. The other part of NVC is to learn how to receive these four pieces of information from the other person regardless of whether they speak a judging language or NVC. If the other person speaks NVC, our life will be a lot easier. They will say these four things with clarity, and our job will be to accurately receive them before we react.

However, if the other person speaks a judging language, then we need to put on NVC ears. [Laughter as Marshall dons a set of NVC ears] NVC ears serve as a translator: No matter what language the other person speaks, when we have these ears on we only hear NVC. For example, the other person says, "The problem with you is ____," with these ears I hear, "What I would like is _____." I hear no judgment, criticism, attack. With these ears on, I realize that all criticism is a pathetic expression of an unmet need, pathetic because it usually doesn't get the person what they want, causing instead all kinds of tension and problems. With NVC, we skip through all that. We never hear a criticism, just unmet needs.

## Listening and Responding in NVC

Now let's practice listening in NVC when certain people speak judgmentally. I would like some people to volunteer their situations so we can all learn from them. If you read what you wrote, we'll see if you answered in NVC or whether some judging language got mixed in. The first question: "What is it that I do that makes life less than wonderful for you?"

Participant A: You appear not to listen.

Marshall: "You appear." Right away I can tell you aren't answering the question in NVC. When you say "you appear," I know a diagnosis is coming up. "You appear to not listen." That's a diagnosis. Have you ever heard one person say, "You don't listen," and the other, "I do too!" "No, you don't!" "Yes, I do!" You see, this is what happens when we start with a criticism rather than an observation. Tell me what I do that makes you interpret me as not listening. I can read the newspaper and watch television while you're talking and still hear you!

Participant A: I'm observing you watching TV.

Marshall: If your partner wasn't listening with NVC, right away he'd hear an attack. But as your partner with NVC ears, I don't hear criticism; I just guess the behavior you are reacting to. "Are you reacting to the fact that I am watching television while you are talking to me?"

Participant A: Yes.

Marshall: "How do you feel when I watch television while you are talking?"
[Marshall adds an aside to participant:] And don't answer, "Not listened to!" That's just a sneaky way of throwing in another judgment.

Participant A: Frustrated and hurt.

Marshall: Now we're cooking! Could you tell me why you feel that way?

Participant A: Because I wanted to feel appreciated.

Marshall: Classical NVC! Notice she didn't say, "I feel frustrated and hurt because you watch television." She doesn't blame me for her feelings, but attributes them to her own needs: "I feel ____ because I ____." People who judge, on the other hand, would express their feelings this way: "You hurt me when you watch television while talking to me. In other words: "I feel ____ because you ____."

Now the fourth question:
"What would you like me to do to make life wonderful for you?"

Participant A: When you are in a conversation, I would appreciate it if you would look into my eyes, as well as tell me back what you heard me say.

Marshall: Okay. Did everybody hear the four things? "When you watch television while I am talking, I feel frustrated and hurt because I would really like some appreciation or attention regarding what I am saying. Would you be willing to look me in the eye while I'm talking and then afterwards repeat back what you heard me say and give me a chance to correct it if it isn't what I meant to say?"

Now of course, the other person may hear it as criticism and will want to defend himself, "I do listen; I can listen while I am watching television." Or if he heard it as a demand, he may do this, "[Sigh] All right." That tells us he didn't hear it as a request, as an opportunity to contribute to our well-being. He heard a demand; he may comply, but if he does, you'll wish he hadn't because he'll be doing it to keep you from freaking out. He'll do it not to make life wonderful for you but to keep life from being miserable for him.

Now that's why marriage is a real challenge. Many people were taught that love and marriage mean denying oneself in doing for the other person. "If I love her, I have to do that, even though I don't want to." So he'll do it, but you'll wish he hadn't.

Participant A: Because he'll keep score.

Marshall: Yeah, people like that have computers in their brains: They'll tell you what happened twelve years ago when they denied themselves. It comes back in one form or another. "After all the times I did things for you when I didn't want to, the least you can do is _____!" Oh yeah, that goes on forever; don't worry, they're excellent statisticians.

# Role-Plays
## *Hearing a Demand*

Another participant: So how does the NVC-er respond when the person says, "I can listen to you and watch at the same time!"

NVC-er: Are you feeling annoyed because you heard some pressure and you would like to be free from pressure?

Participant: Of course, you're always making demands. My God! Demand this, demand that!

NVC-er: So you're kind of exhausted with demands, and you would like to do things because you feel like it and not because you feel pressured?

Participant: Exactly.

NVC-er: Now, I'm feeling very frustrated because I don't know how to let you know what I would like without you hearing it as a demand. I know only two choices: to say nothing and not get my needs met, or to tell you what I would like and have you hear it as a demand. Either way I lose. Could you tell me what you just heard me say?

Participant: Huh?

Now this is very confusing for people who don't know NVC. They grow up in a world of coercion. Their parents might have thought that the only way to get them to do anything is to punish or guilt-trip them. They may not be familiar with anything else. They don't know the difference between a request and a demand. They really believe that if they don't do what the other person wants, the guilt-trip or the threats are going to come out. It is not an easy job for me as NVC-er to help this person hear that my requests are gifts, not demands. When we do succeed, however, we can save ourselves years of misery, because any request becomes misery when people hear it without NVC ears.

NVC-er: I would like to know how I can ask for what I want so it doesn't sound like l am pressuring you.

Participant: I don't know.

NVC-er: Well, I'm glad that we're getting this clear because this is my dilemma: I don't know how to let you know what I want without you immediately hearing either that you have to do it or that I am forcing you to do it.

Participant: Well, I know how much the thing means to you, and . . . if you love somebody, then you do what they ask.

NVC-er: Could I influence you to change your definition of love?

Participant: To what?

NVC-er: Love is not denying ourselves and doing for others, but rather it is honestly expressing whatever our feelings and needs are and empathically receiving the other person's feelings and needs. To receive empathically does not mean that you must comply—just accurately receive what is expressed as a gift of life from the other person. Love is honestly expressing our own needs; that doesn't mean making demands, but just, "Here I am. Here's what I like." How do you feel about that definition of love?

Participant: If I agree with that, I'll be a different person.

NVC-er: Yeah, that's true.

## *Stop Me If I'm Talking "Too Much"*

Marshall: How about another situation?

Next participant (B): Sometimes people say, "I want you to be quiet; I don't want to listen any more," if they are feeling overwhelmed. In a situation where the other person is talking too much . . .

Marshall: If you're an NVC-er, you don't have the words "too much" in your consciousness. To think that there is such a thing as "too much," "just right," or "too little" is to entertain dangerous concepts.

Participant B: What I heard you and the other trainers telling me last night is that I have to stop once in a while to give the other person a chance to respond.

Marshall: "Have to?"

Participant B: No, not "have to." I mean "it would be a good idea to."

Marshall: Yes, you know you don't have to because there have been a lot of times in your life when you haven't. [Laughter]

Participant B: Well, I'd like to get some sort of signal from my friend . . .

Marshall: . . . when he's heard one more word than he wants to hear?

Participant B: Right.

Marshall: The kindest thing we can do is to stop people when they are using more words than we want to hear. Notice the difference: it's not "when they are talking much." I say "kindest" because I have asked several hundred people, "If you are using more words than somebody wants to hear, do you want that other person to pretend that they are listening or to stop you?" Everyone but one person replied adamantly, "I want to be stopped." Only one woman said she didn't know if she could handle being told to stop.

In NVC, we know it's not being kind to the other person to smile and open your eyes wide to hide the fact that your head has gone dead. That isn't helping anybody because the person in front of you becomes a source of stress and strain, and they don't want that. They want every act and every word coming out of their mouth to enrich you. So when it isn't, be kind to them and stop them.

Now it took me awhile to get up the courage to test this out because in the domination culture I grew up in, that's not done. I remember when I first decided to risk this in a social setting. I was working with some teachers in Fargo, North Dakota, and was invited that evening to a social get-together with everybody sitting around talking about stuff. Within ten minutes, my energy had dropped very low. I didn't know where the life was in this conversation or what people were feeling or wanting. One person would say, "Oh, do you know what we did on our vacation?" and then talk about the vacation. Then somebody else talked about theirs. After listening awhile, I gathered up my courage and said: "Excuse me, I'm impatient with the conversation because I'm really not feeling as connected with you as I'd like to be. It would help me to know if you are enjoying the conversation." If they were, I would try to figure out how to enjoy it myself, but all nine people stopped talking and looked at me as if I had thrown a rat in the punch bowl.

For about two minutes I thought I'd die, but then I remembered that it's never the response I receive that makes me feel bad. Since I was feeling bad, I knew I had on my judging ears and was thinking that I had said something wrong. After I put on my NVC ears, I was able to look at the feelings and needs being expressed through the silence and say, "I'm guessing that you're all angry with me and you would have liked for me to have just kept out of the conversation."

The moment I turn my attention to what the other is feeling and needing, already I am feeling better. With my attention there, I totally remove the other person's power to demoralize or dehumanize me or to leave me feeling like PPPPPT (piss poor protoplasm poorly put together). This is true even when, as in this case, I guess wrong. Just because I have NVC ears doesn't mean I always guess right. I guessed they were angry and they weren't.

The first person who spoke told me: "No, I'm not angry. I was just thinking about what you were saying." Then he said, "I was bored with this conversation." And he had been the one doing most of the talking! But this no longer surprises me; I have found that if I am bored, the person doing the talking is probably equally bored. It usually means we are not talking from life: Instead of being in touch with our feelings and needs in this conversation, we're getting into some socially learned habits of boring one another. If you are a middle-class citizen, you are probably so used to it that you don't even know it.

I remember Buddy Hackett saying it wasn't until he was in the Army that he discovered he could get up from a meal without having heartburn. He had been so used to his mother's cooking that heartburn had become a way of life. Likewise, most middle-class people are so used to boredom that it's become a way of life. You just get together and talk from the head; there is no life in it, but it's the only thing you've known. We're dead and don't know it.

When we went around our group, each one of the nine people expressed the same feelings I had: impatient, discouraged that we were there, lifeless, inert . . . then one of the women asked, "Marshall, why do we do this?" "Do what?" "Sit around and bore each other. You're just here tonight but we get together every week and do this!" I said: "Because we probably haven't learned to take the risk that I just did, which is to pay attention to our vitality. Are we really getting what we want from life? If not, let's do something about it. Each moment is precious, too precious, so when our vitality is down, let's do something about it and wake up."

## "What Do You Want From Me?"

Another participant (C): Marshall, I was thinking about how sometimes we women get together with our men and we drive around and say, "Oh, isn't that a cute house" or "Look at that lake, that's the one I want to go on." They think they have to get us a new house or take us to the lake right away, but even though we may seem enthusiastic, we're not asking for anything—we're just talking out loud.

Marshall: Now I want to defend men, and not just men. When you say something and don't say what you want back from others, you create more pain in relationships than you are probably conscious of. Other people have to guess, "Does she want me to say something cute and superficial about this thing, or is she really trying to tell me something else?"

It's like the gentleman sitting next to his wife on the little train at the Dallas airport that connects the terminals. I was sitting across from them. Now this train goes very slowly and the man turned to his wife in a great state of agitation and said, "I have never seen a train go so slow in all of my life." Notice how that is similar to "Isn't that an interesting house?" What did she want there? What does he want here? He wasn't aware of the amount of pain it creates for the other person when we just give commentary and don't make explicit what we want back. It's a guessing game. But knowing what you want back from your words requires a consciousness of living in the moment, of being fully present right now. So he didn't say anything more than, "I've never seen a train go so slow in my whole life."

Sitting right across from them, I could see that she was uncomfortable: somebody she loves is in pain and she doesn't know what he wants. So she did what most of us do when we don't know what a person is wanting from us.

She said nothing. Then he did what most of us do when we're not getting what we want: He repeated himself, as though magically, if you just keep repeating yourself, you'll get what you want. We don't realize that just burns other people's brains out. So again he says, "I have never seen a train go so slow in all of my life!" I loved her response: she said, "They're electronically timed." I don't think that's what he wanted. Why would she give him information that he already knows? Because she is trying to be a fixer, trying to make it better. She doesn't know what to do and he has contributed to her pain by not telling her what he wants. So he repeats himself a third time, "I have never seen a train go so slow in all of my life!" And then she says, "Well, what do you want me to do about it?"

You see, what he wanted is what each of us wants every day, and when we don't get it, there is a significant effect on our morale. We want it every day, usually more than one time a day, and when we don't get it, we pay a high cost. Most of the time when we want it, we're not conscious of it and even if we are conscious of it, we don't know how to ask for it. Tragic. I am confident that what he wanted was empathy. He wanted a response that would tell him that she was in contact with his feelings and needs.

Now if he had studied NVC, he might have said something like: "Boy, I've never seen a train go so slow in all of my life! Could you just reflect back right now what I'm feeling and needing?" She might have said, "So I guess you're really aggravated and you wish they would have managed these trains differently." "Yes, and more than that, you know if we don't get there in time, then we're going to be late and we might have to pay extra for our tickets." "So you're scared and you'd like to get there on time so that we don't have to end up paying more money." "Yeah (sigh)." There is something enormously valuable when we are in pain to just having another person there in contact with it. It's amazing how that kind of attention can make such a difference. It doesn't solve our problem, but it provides the kind of connection that lets the problem solving become more bearable. When we don't get that—as he didn't—then they both end up in more pain than when they started.

## Issues About Food

Another participant (D): Marshall, can I share something that happened last night? I felt bad that my husband couldn't be there for the second night of the partner workshop. I got home at 11:00 PM, and he called at about 11:05 from his motel up in Button Willow, near Bakersfield. I related what happened in the class and what he had missed—the group had discussed eating issues, which were important to me because I'm a compulsive eater. My husband and I had gotten to the point where he didn't even want to discuss food with me because he thought I was killing myself with food. It was so painful for him he wouldn't even talk about it.

So I told him about your suggestion and what had gone on at the workshop and he opened up for the first time in years. When he gets home from teaching, he eats an ice cream to deal with emotions that come from a bad teaching day, and so we were able to actually give each other a lot of empathy over eating as a way to hide from the pain. Then yesterday I got in contact . . . really in contact . . . I wanted an Almond Mocha, so I just imagined the chocolate and the almonds and the crunchy stuff underneath and I thought, *What am I really looking for?* Love! It was just like a flashbulb going off in my head: What I am looking for is love.

Marshall: You wanted some kind of connection with him, and not knowing how to ask for that connection, in the past it might have taken the form of candy.

Participant D: Yes, it was great! We talked for an hour long distance. I think it was a first opening.

Marshall: So two nights in a row you've had a real connection! Now we have to get you talking NVC with yourself and away from thinking that there really such a thing as a "compulsive overeater." You can't say those words in NVC because there are no judgments in NVC. Remember, all judgments are tragic expressions of other things. NVC is a process. When we say anything about ourselves like, "I am a _____," it's static thinking; it puts us in a box and leads to self-fulfilling prophecies. When we think that we (or somebody else) "*is* something," we usually act in a way that makes it happen. There is no verb "to be" in NVC; you can't say, "This person is lazy," "This person is normal," "This person is right." Let's translate "compulsive overeater" into NVC. Use the four things you have already worked with tonight.

Participant D: "Whenever I eat out of my needs to be loved or to be touched. . . ."

Marshall: I feel how?

Participant D: "I feel that the food is assuaging me in a way that . . ."

Marshall: "I feel discouraged . . .?"

Participant D: "I feel discouraged that I am not getting my needs met."

Marshall: "I feel discouraged because I really want to get clear on what my needs are so I can meet them."

Participant D: Yes, right.

Marshall: "So I want to continue doing what I did last night with Bill on the phone. Now when I feel this urge, I want to stop and ask myself, "What do I really need?" You see how we have translated the judgment, "I'm a compulsive overeater" into how I feel, what my unmet needs are, and what I want to do about it. That's how we speak NVC with ourselves.

"When I eat because I want something else . . ." That's the first part, the observation of what she sees herself doing. Secondly she checks her feeling: "I feel discouraged." Number three: "My unmet need is to be in touch with what I really want so I have a chance of getting it." And finally the fourth thing is: "What do I want to do about this to make my most wonderful dream come true? When I start finding myself wanting to eat, I stop and ask myself, 'What is it that I really need?' Then I get in touch with what I really need."

Now she is not thinking of what she is; she's more in touch with a process that moves. That may not solve the problem, but she'll find out by doing it because she isn't thinking of what she is: She is thinking of what she is feeling and wanting and what she is going to do about that. An NVC-er never thinks of herself as a "worthwhile person." If you do, you will spend a good amount of time questioning whether you are a "worthless person." NVC-ers don't spend time thinking about what kind of person they are; they think moment by moment. Not: "What am I?" but "What is the life that is going on in me at this moment?"

## Figuring Out What We Want

Another participant (E): Sometimes we get into doing everything ourselves and are not in touch with how good it may feel to have someone else do for us. While you were talking to her [Participant C above], I thought how nice it was to be in touch with what one needed. Sometimes I just don't know what I need and I get discouraged.

Marshall: Most of us don't know what we want. It's only after we get something and it messes up our life that we know it wasn't what we wanted. I'll say I want an ice cream cone, get one, eat it, then feel terrible and realize that wasn't what I wanted. To an NVC-er, it's not a matter of knowing what is right or wrong. To use the language of life requires courage and choosing what you want based more on intuition than thinking. It's being in touch with your unmet needs and choosing what you want to do about them.

Participant E: I find that I'm a big doer.

Marshall: You just labeled yourself.

Participant E: What I mean is that I run around wanting to connect with people by doing something for them. Sometimes I run across people that don't expect that from me, and it feels so good. But then I start to wonder whether they would really like to receive but just won't let me in.

## When Others Won't Receive

Marshall: That's probably because all their lives they have had people doing things for them and then sending them a bill. It's scary, so now they don't trust you either. They don't realize there is another kind of giving, that there are people who give—not to take care of them—but from the heart.

Participant E: I'm sad I haven't been able to clearly communicate that what I want is to give from the heart. Perhaps I can say to them, "It makes me sad that you don't give me the opportunity to give of myself."

Marshall: If you stop there, then we're back to the man on the train.

Participant E: How about if I add, "Are you willing to tell me if you are willing to give me that opportunity?"

Marshall: Okay, I'm glad that you got that part in. You feel sad because you would really like the opportunity to give to them, to have them receive and feel comfortable with your gift.

Participant E: Right, it's really simple.

## Are We Arguing?

Another participant (F): I feel frustrated when I try to talk with a friend of mine because she tells me she doesn't want to argue. Any time I try to express my feelings and needs, she thinks I'm arguing. She says she doesn't want to argue in front of her kid (who is there all the time).

Marshall: Oh yes, that's a rough one. If a person sees us as trying to argue, then they think that we are trying to win. It's hard to convince them otherwise because people with a judgmental mentality have little idea how you can express feelings and wants without somebody being wrong.

Participant F: But the hard part is she thinks I am arguing even if I try to empathize with her. When I try to guess her feelings and wants, she sees it as "arguing."

Marshall: Because she doesn't want you to judge her. She's afraid once she acknowledges what you say or allows herself to become vulnerable, you are going to zap her and tell her she's wrong for having those feelings and wants.

Participant F: Well, according to her, the reason is that she really doesn't like to deal with this kind of stuff because she just wants the nice parts of life, not all that other heavy stuff.

Marshall: Yes, life is so full of unpleasant stuff as it is, so why deal with anything unpleasant?

Participant F: Yes, right.

Marshall: That's exactly what my dad said at the first workshop that he came to. It's a lovable message, if you look at it that way. But when he first got clear from everybody in the group what a gift it would be to feel pain from their father if their father could just express it—to think of his feelings and needs as a gift—it was a mind-boggler for him. Since that time there have been a lot of radical changes in him.

Certainly many people think that to talk about painful feelings is a negative unpleasant experience because they associate it with guilt games, punishment, and all kinds of other stuff. They haven't seen it as part of an NVC dance and how beautiful it can be to talk about them. When I wrote the first edition of my book, I put in a list of positive feelings and a list of negative feelings. Then I noticed how people think negative feelings are negative. Since that's not what I wanted, in my next edition I put the words "positive" and "negative" in quotes, but that still didn't seem to help. Now I write, "feelings present when our needs are being meet" and "feelings present when our needs are not being met" to show how valuable they both are because they are both talking about life.

So we have some work to do to convince your friend about this.

Marshall as Girlfriend: Look, I don't want to argue. There is enough unpleasantness. Why can't we have a pleasant evening and watch television and enjoy one another?

Participant (would-be NVC-er): So you're feeling irritated . . .

Girlfriend: There you go again! Always talking about feelings!

Participant: [Silence] Uhhh, uhhh.

[Marshall addressing laughter among audience]: So you like seeing this rascal suffer!

Girlfriend: I can't stand it when you do this! (Then she goes into the other room and slams the door.)

Participant G: It's more likely she would throw a lot of words at me and I would just get knocked down for the count. [Laughter]

Marshall: The ten count! Okay, so you play her and come on with those words.

[In the following exchange Participant G plays the role of his girlfriend while Marshall plays Participant F with NVC.]

NVC-er: So you really want to talk . . .

Girlfriend: Stop! Stop! Don't bring this stuff up to me because I don't like it.

NVC-er: I'm feeling very discouraged because I . . .

Girlfriend: Why can't you just be the nice guy, the one I enjoy having a good time with? Let's be loving and forget about this stuff!

NVC-er: So you would like our evening to be light and easy, just enjoying one another.

Girlfriend: Yeah.

NVC-er: I like that part of our relationship too, and I find that comes when we can deal with everything. You see, I want to laugh all my laughter and cry all my tears, and if I cut off half of it, then I find that the other half goes too. That's important. Can you tell me what you heard?

Girlfriend: You are starting in again about feelings and getting depressed. I don't want to hear about it!

NVC-er: So you're really afraid of getting down into those depressed feelings and want to stay out of them.

Girlfriend: Yeah, and besides, tonight with my kid around, I don't want us to argue.

NVC-er: Are you afraid that we are going to fight?

Girlfriend: Please stop!

NVC-er: How would you feel about our continuing this when he is not here?

Girlfriend: Yeah, you can come and meet me for lunch if you want to.

[At lunch:]

NVC-er: I'd like to show you a way that feelings could be very positive regardless of which feelings they are.

Girlfriend: I don't want to hear that stuff . . . have you been taking those workshops again? [Laughter] I want to concentrate on the positive things of life. I don't want to bring up hard feelings. I just want to enjoy the good stuff.

NVC-er: You really want to enjoy life and not get stuck down in some hole talking about negative stuff.

Girlfriend: Yeah, I don't want that stuff in my life. Do you know what happened to Emily today? She went to pick up her boy and couldn't find him anywhere. At first she thought he'd gone home with their neighbor, you know, the Vellas, but then she ran into one of the kids and he told her that he saw her son leaving school at lunch time with a man, a guy he'd never seen. Well, you can imagine how Emily was, especially after that thing that happened to her sister's kid two years ago. Remember? I think I told you about the time her sister was visiting and . . .

NVC-er: Excuse me for interrupting. Are you saying that it's a scary experience to hear things like that happening?

Marshall comments: Do you see what I did? The girlfriend was using more words than I wanted to hear and my energy started to drop, so I interrupted NVC-style to connect with the feelings behind her words in that moment. I am not trying to take the floor away from the other person but to bring life back into the conversation. As I mentioned, my guess is that if I'm bored, so is the other person, so this would be a service to them as well as to me.

NVC-er: You are telling me that it was a real scary experience for you?

Girlfriend: Yeah, he might run into the street and . . .

NVC-er: It really scares you to see just how close we all are to getting the life taken out of us at every moment.

Girlfriend: Don't start that stuff on me again. He was just out in the street and then his mom came after him again . . .

NVC-er: Excuse me, excuse me for interrupting. I'm feeling really impatient because I'm not getting the connection in our conversations that I would like.

Girlfriend: Okay, but I have to go anyway. I've got to go and pick up my kid now. School is going to be out . . .

NVC-er: I'd like you to tell me whether you have any interest in continuing our relationship.

Girlfriend: Sure, you know that I really love and want to be with you.

NVC-er: I really don't know how to continue our relationship, because there are certain things that I need in a relationship that I'm not getting, such as the ability to talk about certain feelings. If that is different from what you want in a relationship, then I would just like to get that clear so that we can have an NVC break-up.

Girlfriend [suddenly speaking NVC]: So you're really feeling frustrated because you want to express your feelings and needs.

NVC-er: That's what I want, but I don't know how you need to be in a personal relationship.

Marshall: There are people who want to keep things at that level, then they have a right to find somebody that wants to stay there with them, but I have never found anybody who really did. Often they have the erroneous idea that I want them to be associating with things in the past that are painful. Usually I am able to show them the difference between what they think I am talking about and what I am really talking about. With this particular girlfriend, I might have to be very clever to get that in because she wasn't giving me much space.

## Hearing No

Another Participant (H): I know that NVC is about figuring out my needs and requesting for what I want, but that doesn't work with my boyfriend. If I start asking him for what I want, he'll just get real angry and huffy. Then I'll tell him to act decently or maybe wish I hadn't mentioned any of it in the first place.

Marshall: It's amazing how it just turns people into beasts when they hear that word. They beast themselves and they beast the speaker and it's a very small word—only two letters. Can anybody guess what the word is?

Lots of participants: "No!"

Marshall: Yeah. It's amazing how people are so frightened of this word that they are afraid to ask for what they want, because what if the other person says "no?" I tell them it's not the "no" that bothers them, and they say, "Yes, it is; I'm so afraid of it." The problem is never the 'no," but what we tell ourselves when the person says "no." If we tell ourselves that it is a rejection, that's a problem because it hurts. Rejection, ugh. Of course, if we have NVC ears on, we would never hear "no." We are aware that a "no" is just a sloppy expression of what a person wants. We don't hear the slop; we just hear the want. It takes some practice.

Marshall [addressing Participant H]: So how did this boyfriend say "no" to you?

Participant H: Well, I asked for something and he goes "NO!" And so I said . . .

Marshall: With that kind of energy already we know what the problem is. He heard what, folks?

Participants: Demand.

Marshall: He heard a demand. Whenever people say "no" like that, they're scared to death that their autonomy is going to be taken away. They're afraid that if they really hear what the other person wants, they're going to get sucked up and have to do it whether they want to or not. So when a person says "no" like that, we know that they didn't hear our request. It has nothing to do with us; it's obviously not a rejection because they didn't even hear the request they heard demand.

Participant H: So at this point I tried guessing what he was feeling, and he goes: "I just want you to understand, to get it. I don't want to play this game and I don't have to. I just want you to get the fact that the answer is no."

Marshall (role-playing the boyfriend): "Just realize how scared I am about having my autonomy taken away."

It's so very precious for us to be able to do things when we choose to do them—not because somebody we love has to have it or they're going to freak out, or because they are going to keep talking at us until we do. People are very scared of spending so much of their lives having to give when it's not from the heart. So they're very reactive. He says: "Just get it! Just understand. I just do not want to do this today. I just need to protect my autonomy."

From the tone of your boyfriend's voice when he says, "I

just want you to get it," he has a serious case of the sick-of-dependency, not-yet-autonomous blues. So what do you say next to him?

Participant H: I . . . I just rolled over and went to sleep. [Laughter] Well, I kind of yelled and screamed, "No, no, no!" I got angry, really fierce, and said, "I'm very upset." And he goes, "Oh, good, you've got life in you." [Laughter] And then he got silent.

Marshall: You know that he was really scared. He doesn't feel he can protect himself against you. You were very tense, and he knows to withdraw and protect himself.

Participant H: What can I do in this case? Just go "under-the-hat" [give oneself empathy] with myself?

Marshall: The most important thing, of course, is for you not to think that this has anything to do with you.

Participant H: Yeah, I was okay with that.

Marshall: Then that's about the best I know to do in a situation when somebody says "no" to my needs: making sure I don't think there is anything wrong with my needs. I need to really work fast because, with that intensity and pain, I could make a mistake and think there is something wrong with my needs if they can scare a person that much.

Participant H: Well, I just would have liked to have heard what he wanted.

Marshall: He is all tied up in protecting his autonomy: That's what he wants. He needs space to just feel safe in the relationship, to know he's not going to get sucked up into something before he is ready.

Participant H: So I can kind of give myself empathy silently. Keep quiet.

Marshall: Yeah. Just be aware if he's like most men—if my wife is right—he'll need about three incarnations to get past that. [Laughter] So in the meantime, go and get some women friends and just don't aggravate yourself. My wife once said about the best one-liner I've ever heard; she said to me, "You could read demands into a rock." [Laughter] I said, "Guilty as charged."

## Do You Want to Hear This?

Again Participant G: When he's having his sick-of dependency and not-yet autonomous blues, I get really desperate because I want him to know that, in fact, I can't make him do anything, so he doesn't need to worry about that at all. If he could just trust that, we could have a lot more fun. Do you hear what my pain is?

Marshall: Only when he feels that you can fully empathize with how frightening it is for him to be in a close relationship and that might take a long time then, maybe, he can start to understand how frustrating it is for you to have needs and not be able to express them without having him turn them into demands.

Participant G: Is there some way I can effectively communicate to him how much I want him to understand that I can't make him do anything?

Marshall: You can try. This person will hear anything as a demand, even or perhaps particularly, your silence, so you might as well have some fun screaming. If you keep your needs hidden inside, he's going to carry that as a very heavy burden. Screaming what you have to say a few thousand times might get him to understand.

Participant G: I was concerned about doing the inner work on my own without saying anything to him because he may be thinking I am avoiding the issue by not talking about it.

Marshall: Yes, how painful it is not to be able to say our needs. There's nothing wrong with screaming, "I would like you to tell me what I have to do or say for you to trust that I never want to get you into anything that is painful for you," while also empathizing with just how frightened he may be, having grown up in a family where he's been told he's wrong. He has been through all kinds of games so he needs a lot of time and patience to gain that trust. I don't think it's going to happen just by your telling him that you won't ever make him do anything. He needs a lot of empathy due to the scare from his prior experiences.

## Expressing Feelings and Needs

Marshall: Who's got another one?

Participant H: It's a telephone call. He says: "Hi, I'm not going to be able to come today. My daughter's school is getting out at 1:30 and I want to spend quality time with you and I will be nervous if we get together."

Marshall: And then you say?

Participant H: I was able to identify my feelings. "I have pain in my heart." That's what I said.

Marshall: "I have pain in my heart."

Participant H: Yeah, but I wasn't able to identify my needs.

Marshall: But you weren't able to say what your needs were, and your timing was a bit judgmental. This person needs empathy, and the first thing they hear is "pain in your heart." So we already have a nice fight about to start here.

Participant H: When I said I had pain in my heart, he asked, "Why?"

Marshall: I've asked people in several countries, "What are the hardest messages for you to hear and really feel safe?' "Why" questions top the list. If you really want to scare people, ask "why" questions. "Why?"

Participant H: Silence, I said nothing. Then he listed a whole bunch of other reasons why he wasn't able to come.

Marshall: This poor suicidal guy. He doesn't realize that when you try to explain and justify, it just sounds like an attack to the other person. So then what?

Participant H: I said, "I have pain in my heart, and I have to think about that." And then I thought, *I am going to call some of my NVC friends.*

Marshall: Ahh . . . now there's a smart thing to do! Okay, so if I understand this, you really wanted to be with this person.

Participant H: Yes.

Marshall: And this person's needs were in conflict with yours. This person was saying, "I have other needs right now, other than to meet your needs."

Participant H: Right, and logically I could understand that, but in my heart . . .

Marshall: In your head you could understand it, but you have the pain in your heart because you heard what?

Participant H: I heard, "You don't want to be with me."

Marshall: Yes, you heard a rejection. That's how to make life really miserable. When somebody's needs are in conflict with ours and they say, "I'd like to do something else right now rather than to meet your needs," you hear that as saying that they don't want to be with you. You have nicer language, you say "pain in my heart." I must confess, I have been known to wear judging ears when I hear a "no" myself. It's very hard to put on NVC ears when you hear a "no."

Yes, by all means, let's learn how to put on NVC ears in such a situation because that can save us a lot of misery. If we hear another person's needs being different from ours as a rejection, we will soon be rejected. Who wants to be around someone who reads rejection each time your needs arc in conflict with theirs? That gets very heavy very quickly. So unless we learn to put on NVC ears, we will in fact drive the other person away. I realize that this is not always easy, but when we learn to put on NVC ears . . . [Marshall puts on a pair of fuzzy NVC ears to chuckles from the audience, and responds to the laughter by saying:] I feel very hurt. [More laughter]

Participant: Your ears aren't working then.

Marshall: Ahhhhhh! [Lots more laughter] Yes, these are faulty ears, obviously. I need to get another pair.

Now, as soon as I put on these ears, a miracle takes place: Rejection vanishes from the earth. I never hear a "no." I never hear a "don't want." Judgments and criticism vanish from the earth. Then all I hear is the truth, which to an NVC-speaking person is this: All that other people are ever expressing are their feelings and needs. The only things that people are ever saying, no matter how they are expressing it, are how they are and what they would like to make life even better. When a person says "no," that's just a poor way of letting us know what they really want. We don't want to make it worse by hearing a rejection: We hear what they want.

Some of you have heard me tell about the woman who said to her husband, "I don't want you spending so much time at work." Then she got furious with him when he signed up for a golf tournament. [Laughter] She had told him what she didn't want, and he didn't have NVC ears on. He didn't know how to hear what she did want. Of course, it would have made it easier if she had said what she did want. But if he would have had NVC ears, when she said, "I don't want you spending so much time at work," he would have said:

Husband: Oh, so you're concerned about my well-being and you want me to get more recreation?

Wife: Not on your life. You have spent only two nights in the last six months with the children and me.

Husband: Ah, so you're really disappointed in how much time we spend together, and you'd like me to spend at least one night a week with you and the children?

Wife: Exactly.

You see, with NVC ears we never hear what a person doesn't want. We try to help them get clear what they do want. Being clear only about what we don't want is a dangerous phenomenon. It gets us into all kinds of confusion.

When we are clear on what we do want from other people, especially when we are clear about what we want their reasons to be in doing something, then it becomes clear to us that we can never get our needs met through any kind of threats or punitive measures. Whether we are parents, teachers, or whatever, we never get our needs met by punishment. No one who is the least bit conscious is going to want anyone to do anything for us out of fear, guilt, or shame. We're NVC-oriented enough to see into the future, to see that any time anyone does anything out of fear, guilt, or shame, everybody loses. So we need to put the NVC ears on now, and give this person some empathy. Let's try it again.

Marshall as Partner: I have a real conflict. I would really like to be with you when I can be conscious and give you my full attention, but today my attention is distracted by my daughter.

Participant H: Do you want me to be an NVC-er?

Marshall: Yeah, put these ears on. [hands participant a pair of NVC ears, which she dons]

Participant H (as herself): I'm really disappointed.

Marshall: No, no. This poor person needs empathy.

Participant H (as herself): So you'd really like to spend some quality time with me, when you can be fully in my presence without distraction, but today you need to attend to your daughter because she's getting out of school early.

Marshall as Partner: Yes, thank you for giving me that empathy, because you see, I have this real fear that if I don't always meet the needs of the person I care for, they're going to take it as a rejection, and that I'm going to be rejected and abandoned. So it's very terrifying for me to tell you that my needs are in conflict with yours. I've had terrible experiences like that in my background, where when I don't do what everybody else wants, I don't get the love that I want. It's just terrifying for me to tell you that my needs are in conflict with yours. I was afraid you'd hear, "I don't want to be with you."

Participant H (as herself): You want some more empathy.

Marshall as Partner: Yeah, I want some more empathy.

Participant H (as herself): I guess you were scared that you were not going to be able to spend time with me today because you're feeling a need to attend to your daughter. And you're afraid that by telling me that, I may think that you don't want to spend time with me. In the past, you've had many experiences and times you have wanted to fill the needs of a person you care for, but when you have had a conflict, or haven't been able to do that, the other person heard that you didn't want to spend time with them. When they felt rejected, they punished you, and then you felt guilt and shame. They judged you and you felt even more guilty and scared.

Marshall as Partner: Yes, yes . . . it feels so good to get this empathy, the heck with my daughter, I'm coming over! [Laughter and applause] Now I can even hear you when you start to tell me about the pain in your heart because I got my empathy first.

Participant H (as herself): Now I'm wondering if you'd like to hear how I'm feeling about this.

Marshall as Partner: Yeah, I'd like to hear how you are feeling.

Participant H (as herself): I'm feeling really disappointed.

Marshall as Partner: Oh, I'm sorry; I didn't mean to disappoint you.

Marshall: Now watch out. He has learned suicidal tendencies to take responsibility for other people's feelings. As soon as she said she was disappointed, he went on alert. Without NVC, when people hear somebody in pain, immediately they feel that they have done something wrong and now they have to do something about it. And so this person is doing the number one thing that people unfamiliar with NVC do: apologize. You know that there is a judgment coming soon when you hear these words: "I'm sorry." Then he repeats a whole lot of excuses that you don't want to hear about why it's so important for him to be with the daughter today, leaving you in all that pain, not getting any empathy.

Marshall as Partner: I'm sorry, I didn't mean to disappoint you, but this is the only day . . . blah-blah blah . . . excuses, excuses, justification, etc." Phew!! [Laughter]

Participant H: Is this empathy time?

Marshall: No, scream in NVC! You gave them empathy; now get empathy back.

Participant H (as herself): Okay. Well, I'm having a need to share my feelings with you right now.

Marshall as Partner: Yes, it's important that you do.

Participant H (as herself): What I'd like to do right now is tell what I'm feeling and then when I'm done, maybe you could tell me back what I've said?

Marshall as Partner: Oh yes, I have a very bad habit I don't listen very well. I've never been able to listen too well. My mother was not a very good listener either, and, uh, you know . . . [Laughter]

Participant A: Next time will I talk to his mom?

Marshall: No, just scream in NVC.

Participant H (as herself): I hear that you have some pain around this.

Marshall: No, don't give him even that much empathy; just scream in NVC.

Participant A (as herself): I have a need to share my feelings and my needs about this with you, and I would really like you to listen to what I have to say, and afterward I'd like you to tell me what I said. Okay?

Marshall as Partner: Yeah. [Marshall is making gestures . . . The audience laughs while Participant H asks Marshall:]

Participant H: Did you talk to him ahead of time? (More laughter)

Marshall: I've even got his expressions down pat!

Participant H (as herself): I'm feeling really disappointed when I hear that you're not going to be able to spend the day with me.

Marshall as Partner: Yes, but . . .

Marshall playing NVC Coach to partner: Shh, shh, just hear her out.

Marshall as himself, speaking to group: Sometimes you need to have an emergency NVC coach to help out.

Participant H (as herself): I was really looking forward to spending the day with you because I enjoy your company so much and I was needing to see you.

Marshall enacts dialogue between judging puppet (partner) and NVC puppet (coach):

NVC Coach: Can you tell her back what she said?

Partner: Yes, I understand how she feels.

NVC Coach: Could you just say what she feels?

Partner: No, she's right, she has every right to feel that way. It was terrible of me. I should never have made the promise if I knew that I may not have been able to do it. It was terrible of me. I just feel terribly guilty.

NVC Coach: Are you aware that when you hear what she said as a judgment of yourself, that it is a further violation of her?

Partner: Huh?

NVC Coach: When you're hearing what another person says as meaning you did something wrong, that's a further violation of the other person because then, not only are they not getting the understanding that they need, now they get the feeling that their honesty creates problems for you. It's going to be harder for her to be honest in the future if she tries to tell what's going on with her and you think that you did something wrong.

Partner: But I'm not wearing NVC ears; I can't hear anything except that I did something wrong.

NVC Coach: You want some NVC ears?

Partner: Yes! [Laughter as Marshall puts NVC ears on the judging partner puppet]

Partner: So you're really feeling disappointed because I . . .

NVC Coach: No, you didn't have the ears on straight. No, she's not feeling disappointed because of such and such. Quit taking responsibility for her feelings. Just hear what is going on in her.

Marshall as NVC Partner: So you feel disappointed because you were looking forward to this, and you really wanted to spend that time with me.

Participant H (as herself): Yes!

Partner (with new NVC ears): It's something you were really looking forward to.

Participant H (as herself): Yeah. I really enjoyed hearing you say that!

Partner: It really feels good when you can get that empathy?

Participant H (as herself): Yes, it feels real good.

Partner: And you don't want me to feel like a worm?

Participant H (as herself): No, I don't want you to feel like a worm.

Partner: You just needed this empathy?

Participant H (as herself): Yeah!

Partner: And that's all I have to do?

Participant H (as herself) [with new softness in her voice]: Yes, and I'm feeling really grateful to you for hearing that.

Partner: That's amazing! I always thought that I had to do everything that everyone else wanted me to in order to be loved. The idea that people just want my empathy and then my honesty . . . this is astonishing! Thank you for staying with me. I'll try to keep these ears on all the time.

Participant H: I'd enjoy that!

Marshall: The first thing to do when we start to get angry or defensive is to recognize that we didn't hear the other person. What breaks us out of these fights is our consciousness. If we hear anything but a gift in the other person's message, we didn't hear them. You have to notice when your NVC ears have fallen off. Anger is a wonderful clue; it's like a wake-up call to a NVC-er. As soon as I get angry or defensive or hear an attack or demand, I know that I didn't hear the other person. Instead of connecting to what's going on in them, I'm up in my head judging that they're wrong in some way. If I'm using NVC, I know to shut up as quickly as possible, put my NVC ears on, and listen to myself. I've wounded myself if I have judging ears. How do I do this?

I listen to myself. I give myself empathy. I see how much pain I've created for myself by putting on my judging ears and hearing all of that. I notice that this has happened and then I shut up and enjoy the show going on in my head. It's just like watching a movie. [Laughter]

## Reassurance

Participant I: I need to know the difference between empathizing with someone by saying, "It sounds like you're scared and need some reassurance" and actually reassuring them. What if they say, "Yes, I do need some reassurance."

Marshall: If the person says that they want reassurance, and I can give it to them willingly, there's no problem. The problem is giving them that reassurance when they want empathy. For example, one time my oldest daughter was looking in the mirror and she said, "I'm as ugly as a pig." I said, "You're the most gorgeous creature God ever put on the face of this earth." She said, "Daddy!" and she goes out and slams the door. I was being judgmental there. She wanted empathy and in order to meet my own needs, I tried to fix her. What did I do? I went into the other room after judging myself a bit, saying, "You preach about this every day of the year, and then when it happens, you forget. You forget the Buddha's advice: 'Don't fix it, just be there.' After that, I went to her and said,

Marshall: I'm guessing you needed to hear how disappointed you were with your appearance and not my reassurances.

Daughter: That's right. You always try to fix everything. [Laughter]

Marshall: Guilty as charged.

## Talking About It in Public

Another Participant (I): Sometimes I feel like I'm taking care of my mate's feelings. In the past I'd sometimes say something that he considered private or personal to another couple or in a group. I've since gotten clear on the difference between his stuff and my stuff, but occasionally there is a fine line between what I can and can't say. So I'm wondering, when we are in a group of people, when it would be appropriate and not "co-dependent" to ask him, "Is it okay if I talk about this?" Sometimes when I ask and he says no, or says I shouldn't have said something, I feel angry and censored. Do you get my question?

Marshall: I think I do. Let me see. You're saying that sometimes it's not clear to you when your mate is comfortable with your talking about things with other people and when he's not.

Participant I: Yeah.

Marshall: You've put your question in a non-NVC form and are heading in a direction that is dangerous. I cleaned it up for you and translated it into NVC. In the book, *Revolution in Psychiatry*, Ernst Becker, an anthropologist, suggests that depression results from cognitively arrested alternatives. He means that by asking yourself questions of the sort you started with, we fill our head with unanswerable questions. "Is it okay?" "Is it appropriate?" Those questions usually cannot be answered and we end up spinning in our heads. You notice I translated those questions. You're saying that sometimes your partner is uncomfortable with some things you say. It doesn't mean it's not okay for you to do it. It doesn't mean that it's inappropriate. It just means he doesn't like it. You're just asking your partner: "I'm not clear what those things are. Can you give me an example of some of the things that you would like or wouldn't like for me to say?"

Marshall as Partner: Well, obviously I don't want you to say inappropriate things to other people. [Laughter]

Marshall: We need to get clear on the difference between emotional slavery, obnoxiousness, and liberation. Emotional slavery is as far from NVC as you can get. It's when the person thinks that they have to do everything that others think is appropriate, right, normal. They spend all of their lives thinking that they have to please other people and guess what other people think is appropriate. This is a heavy load. For example, someone comes home upset about something; it doesn't make any difference what it is.

Marshall as Partner: I'm upset about everything.

Marshall as Judging Person: Oh, here, eat some chicken soup.

Marshall: You see, it doesn't matter what it is. As soon as a person is in pain, then the other thinks they have to scurry around and take care of them. Then they come out to an NVC workshop, and I'm not totally coherent in explaining how "we are not responsible for other people's feelings,"—I fail to make clear what we are responsible for. They go home from the workshop and when their partner says, "I'm still upset about A," they respond: Well, that's your problem; I'm not responsible for your feelings. [Laughter]

Partner: Where did you learn that?

Participant: At an NVC workshop.

Partner: I'm going to go kill those people!

The NVC concept is, "No, we are not responsible for other people's feelings, but we're conscious that we don't have to keep rebelling against them, saying things like, "I'm not responsible for your feelings." We can just hear what the other person is feeling and not lose our center. We can hear what they want and give them empathy, but we don't have to do what they want."

We make it clear that we need empathy, not the other person giving up or giving in. To hear and respect what the other person needs doesn't mean that you must do what they ask. Does that answer your question or did I go astray? You need to get very clear on what you need. Without NVC, we say, "May I?" "Is it okay?" NVC-ers never want approval from other people. NVC-ers never give that power away and have other people tell them what to do. This is what we'd say in NVC:

Here's what I want. I'd like to know where you stand in relationship to that. I want to know your needs as well as mine, not because when I hear your needs I am going to give mine up or give in. I am conscious that I cannot benefit at your expense. Your needs are equally as important to me as my needs. And I'm clear that doesn't ever mean having to give up my needs.

## I Lose Myself Around You

Another Participant (K): Are you ready for another one? They say: "I can't be in a long-term relationship. I lose myself around you. I'm not emotionally mature enough. I can see now that I was undergoing aberrant behavior in getting involved and agreeing to your wanting a long-term relationship. Something was wrong with me that led me to think that I could so quickly fall in love." I told her, "I'd still like to be your friend." And she said, "I don't know what to say."

Marshall: Yes, yes, this person has been taught non-NVC concepts of love such as, "If you really love somebody, you deny your needs and take care of them." Then as soon as this person gets into a close relationship—a loving relationship—they turn judgmental. Until then they're lovely, they're wonderful. These are the most dangerous judges because they're really judges in NVC clothing. [Laughter] You see, in the early stage of the relationship, they are giving from the heart, they enjoy giving; it's easy, they don't think of it until they pass the line.

What is the line? It's when people fear that they've "made a commitment." If you really want to scare them to death, talk about commitment, or use the word "serious." As soon as they think it's a "serious relationship," or the word love" comes up—"I love this person."—you're going to get killed. The moment they define it as a serious relationship, that's when they feel like they are responsible for your feelings. For to show love, they have to deny themselves and do for you.

All of that is behind the statements: "I lose myself in a relationship with you. I can't stand it. I see your pain and I lose me, and I need to get away from it all." At least they are taking responsibility for it. At a more primitive level, they would have put it all on you: "You're too dependent. You're too needy." That's seriously deranged. They are not aware of their own internal dynamic.

Marshall as Partner: I'm really scared to be in the relationship because I just close down. As soon as I see that you have any need or any pain, I just can't tell you the pain that I feel and then I start to feel like I'm in prison. I feel like I'm being smothered and so I just have to get out of this relationship as soon as possible.

As an NVC-er, I have to do a lot of work with that, but I don't think that there is something wrong with my needs or my love. If I did, that would make a bad situation doubly bad. I need not take responsibility for this. I need to truly hear what you are saying.

So, you're in a panic. It's very hard for you to hold on to the deep caring and love that we've had without making of it responsibility and duty and obligation closing down your own freedom, and feeling like you have to take care of me.

Partner: Exactly! It's just like a prison. I can hardly breathe.

NVC-er: As soon as you hear my pain or my feelings, it's just as if your life stops.

Partner: Yeah! [sighs]

NVC-er: I'm really glad that you are telling me this. Would it be safer if we defined ourselves as friends rather than lovers?

Partner: I do this with friends, I do it with anybody that I care for. I did this with my dog once. [Laughter]

NVC-er: Gosh, I'm in such a dilemma here. I'd like to express my pain in relationship to that, but then if I express my pain, I'm afraid you'll freak.

Partner: Yes, I will. I will. As soon as you express any pain, I think that I have done something wrong and that I have to do something about it. My life is over: I have to take care of you.

Then to myself I say: "Wow, how painful it is for me not to be able to get any empathy. To have someone receive my feelings and needs all that is alive in me, that I would like to be a gift to someone; turning my needs into demands is painful to me. I do not know how to get what I need from this person. Let me try one more time to see if I can get empathy from this person."

Marshall as NVC-er: Would you be willing to try to hear just one message from me without taking responsibility for it?

Partner: What do you mean?

NVC-er: I'd like to tell you a feeling and a need, and have you hear only that and nothing else. Not to hear that you have to do anything about it. Not to hear that you did anything wrong. Just repeat back what you hear me say. Would you be willing to do that?

Partner: I'll try.

NVC-er: I feel so sad . . .

Partner: I'm sorry. [Laughter]

NVC-er: Please don't. Just wait, hold on, and repeat what I say. I feel sad because I would like my feelings and my needs to be gifts to you and not a threat. Could you tell me what you heard me say?

Partner: That I shouldn't react so strongly.

NVC-er: No, I'm really not trying to tell you what you should or shouldn't do. I have a feeling and a need: just concentrate on that. I feel very sad because I would like my feelings and my needs to be a gift to you and not such a threat. Can you tell me what you heard me say?

Partner: That I make you sad.

NVC-er: You don't make me sad; my needs make me sad. Can you just hear that?

Partner: Say it again.

NVC-er: I feel very sad, because I would really like it if my feelings and needs could be a gift to you and not a threat.

Partner: You feel sad because I . . .

NVC-er: No!

Partner: Because you . . . ?

NVC-er: Thank you.

Partner: Because you would like your feelings and needs to be a gift to me and not a threat.

NVC-er: I'm grateful that you heard that. Go in peace, and I hope some day you can come back and enjoy me.

## Making a Request

Participant K: But there's the next sentence. [Laughter]

Marshall: What's that?

Participant K (as himself): I feel scared; I need to feel we are still connected because we were connected. It doesn't necessarily matter how we are connected. I don't need you as a special partner, but I still need to feel we are connected and that we are friends.

Marshall: That's wonderful as far as you've gone, but if you stop there, it's not NVC. What you've stated is your feeling and your unmet need to still maintain contact with her, but you didn't make clear at the very end exactly what you want the other person to do. For a person that hears the way this one does, that will be fuel to the fire. When you say to a person without NVC ears, "Be a friend," and you don't make it clear what you are wanting from them, they'll read in again: "You want to smother me. You want me to be your slave." You must be very concrete with people who don't speak NVC. You cannot say: "I want you to love me. I want your understanding. I need you to listen. I need you to be a friend." Concretely, what exactly do you want this person to do to be your friend?

Participant K (as himself): I would like to call you at least once a month and check in on how you are and let you know how I am.

Marshall: What you need to say right now is, "I'd like you to tell me if you would be willing to have me call once a month to check in."

Marshall as Participant's Partner: For how many minutes?

Participant K (as himself): Oh, about thirty minutes on a Sunday.

Marshall: Yes.

We need to be that concrete with NVC.

## Dealing With Sexism or Racism

Another participant (L): [Speaking softly] I know someone who said that, when a woman gets married, she turns into a bitch.

Marshall: Now, without NVC, we would quickly interpret that as a sexist remark. However, with such a thought in our head, we lose the power to get this person to be more sensitive to our needs. As soon as we judge someone as "sexist" or "racist," even if we don't say the judgment out loud, but just carry it in our head, we have almost no power to get what we need . . . and now you said what?

Participant L: I paused because I was upset and didn't know what to say. I didn't tell him it was a sexist comment. During the pause, I felt the pain of men telling women things like that, and I wasn't in the mood to use NVC.

Marshall: That few-second pause used up all your NVC energy. Then you gave yourself permission to not use NVC.

Participant L: I shook my head and said, "Women should have permission to be bitchy."

Marshall: You're agreeing. An NVC-er never agrees or disagrees. I warn you: Never go up to a persons head—it's ugly up there. [Laughter] Stay away from their head. Let's go to their heart.

Marshall as Man: Is it true that all you women turn into bitches when you get married?

NVC-er: [Silence]

This is the pause. The NVC-er is very angry right now. As I told you earlier, when the NVC-er gets angry, it knows that it didn't hear what it needs to hear. So she sits back and enjoys the judgment show that is going on in her head for a few moments.

NVC-er [internal dialog]: I'd like to take his sexist neck and wring it. I'm sick and tired of these remarks. I'm sick and tired of what I call insensitivity to my needs. Why, just because I am a woman, do I have to have this kind of talk thrown at me at work all the time! Sigh. [Internal dialog ends]

[Out loud] Are you feeling some tension about things going on in your marriage that you want to talk about? [Lots of laughter]

Participant L: Actually, I really thought that at the time but I didn't choose to bring that up because we were having a farewell lunch for one of the employees at work.

Marshall as Man: What are you talking about? We were just having fun. You take everything so sensitively.

Marshall as NVC-er: So you were just playing with me and would have liked me to be able to enjoy that?

Man: Yeah.

NVC-er: Well, I'd like to tell you why that is not easy for me to do. I'd like to tell you how painful it is when I hear comments like that.

Man: Well, you shouldn't be so sensitive.

NVC-er: I'd like you to wait till I finish talking before you jump in and tell me what I shouldn't do. Would you be willing to do that?

Man: Touchy, touchy! [Laughter]

NVC-er: So you're really feeling hurt and you would like me to be able to play with you.

Man: Yeah, you liberals are really a pain in the ass to be around.

NVC-er: So you would like to be able to just joke and play and not have to worry about every word?

Man: Yeah.

NVC-er: And I'd like to be able to do that too, but I'd like you to understand why that is so painful for me to do. I'd like you to tell me if you would be willing to hear what goes on in me.

So now I educate him.

## Name-calling

Another Participant: How does an NVC-er react to forceful name-calling?

Marshall: In NVC, all names are tragic expressions of unmet needs. An NVC-er asks himself, when the names are coming at him, "What is this person wanting that they're not getting?" Tragically, they don't know any other way of saying the need except to call the name.

Marshall as Name-caller: You're too sensitive!

NVC-er: You would like me to understand you differently?

Name-caller: You're the most selfish person I've ever met.

NVC-er: You would have liked me to save that last piece of cake for you?

Names are simply tragic expressions of unmet needs. NVC-ers know that there is no such thing as normal, abnormal, right, wrong, good, or bad. They know that all of those are a product of language that trained people to live under a king. If you want to train people to be docile to a higher authority, to fit into hierarchical structures in a subservient way, it is very important to get people up in their head and to get them thinking what is "right," what is "normal," what is "appropriate," and to give that power to an authority at the top who defines what those are. You can get my booklet on Social Change if you want to learn more about how this came about.

When a person is raised in that culture, they have this tragic trick played on them. When they are hurting the most and needing the most, they don't know how to express it except by calling names to other people.

With NVC we want to break that cycle. We know that the basis of violence is when people are in pain and don't know how to say that clearly. There is a book called *Out of Weakness* by Andrew Schmookler of the Conflict Resolution Department at Harvard University. He has written in this book that violence—whether we are talking about verbal, psychological, or physical violence, between husband and wife, parents and children, or nations—all violence at the base is people not knowing how to get in touch with what is inside. Instead, they are taught a language that indicates that there are villains out there, bad guys out there that are causing the problem. Then you have a country where even the leader will say of another country: "They're the evil empire." And then the leaders of the other country will say back, "These are imperialist oppressors," instead of seeing and revealing the pain, fear, and unmet needs behind the other's words. This is a very dangerous social phenomenon. That's why NVC-ers are committed to just hearing the pain and needs behind any name—not to take it in and not to respond in kind.

# Expressing Appreciation

Another Participant (M): Could you please say the three things that you need to express an appreciation?

Marshall: The three things we need to express appreciation—not praise, because there is no such thing as praise in NVC. Praise is a classical judging technique; managers love it because they say research shows that employees perform better if you praise them at least once a day. That does work for a while until the employees see the manipulation in it. We never give appreciation in NVC to try to create some result in the other person. We only give it to celebrate, to let the other person know how great we feel about something that they have done. The three things are:

1. What the other person has done that we appreciate, and we are very specific about that,
2. Our feelings, and
3. Our needs that have been fulfilled.

# What Does It Take to Practice NVC?

Another Participant (N): Marshall, I would also like you to mention the three things that it takes to become proficient at NVC.

Marshall: First of all, the good news is that it doesn't require us to be perfect. It does not require us to be saints. And we don't have to be patient. We don't have to have positive self-esteem; we don't have to have self-confidence. I have demonstrated that you don't even have to be a normal person. [Laughter]

What does it take? First and foremost, spiritual clarity. We have to be highly conscious how we want to connect with human beings. We're living in a society, I'm afraid to say, that is largely judgmental in its history and evolution. It's leaning toward NVC, very rapidly, if you listen to Teilhard Chardin. He was a paleontologist who thinks in terms of tens of thousands of years, but it's not moving as fast as I'd like, so I'm doing what I can to speed it up. The main thing I'm trying to do is work on myself. When I get myself fully engaged with NVC, I think I am helping the planet; then what energy I have left over, I use to try to help other people become engaged with NVC. So the most important thing is spiritual clarity, that we be highly conscious of how we want to connect with people. For me, I have to stop every day—two, three, four times—really stop, and remind myself how I want to connect with other people in this world.

How do I do that? This is individual for everyone. Some people call it meditation, prayer, stopping and slowing down, whatever you call it. I do it differently every day myself, but it's basically just stopping and slowing down and doing a check on what is running through my head. Are judgments running through my head? Is NVC running through my head? I stop and look at what is going on in there and slow down. I remind myself of the "subtle sneaky important reason why I was born a human being and not a chair," to use a line from one of my favorite plays, *A Thousand Clowns*. So that's the most important thing: spiritual clarity.

Second: practice, practice, practice. I make a note every time I catch myself judging myself or other people. I make a note of what was the stimulus for this. What did I do? What did others say or do that, all of a sudden, I gave myself permission to turn back into judgment? Then I use that. Some time in the day I sit and look at my list, and I try to give myself empathy for the pain that was going on in me at the time. I try not to beat myself up. I try to hear what pain was going on in me that led me to speak in that way. Then I ask myself: "How could I have used NVC in that situation? What might the other person have been feeling and needing?" Now, NVC-ers love to mess things up because an NVC-er doesn't try to be perfect. We know the danger of trying to be perfect. We just try to become progressively less stupid. [Laughter] When your objective is to become progressively less stupid, every time you mess something up, it becomes cause for a celebration. It gives you a chance to learn how to be less stupid. So practice, practice, practice learning how to be less stupid.

And third, it really helps to be part of an NVC support community. We are living in a judgmental world and it helps to create an NVC world around us from which we can now start to build a greater world an NVC world. That is why I am so grateful that we have all of the NVC teams locally.

## What Love's Got to Do With It

It may help you to understand that Nonviolent Communication really grew from my attempt to understand the concept of love and how to manifest it, how to *do* it. I had come to the conclusion that love is not just something we feel, but it is something we manifest, something we do, something we have. And **love is something we give:** We give of ourselves in particular ways. It's a gift when you reveal yourself nakedly and honestly, at any given moment, for no other purpose than to reveal what's alive in you. Not to blame, criticize, or punish. Just "Here I am, and here is what I would like. This is my vulnerability at this moment." To me, that giving is a manifestation of love.

Another way we give of ourselves is through how we receive another person's message. It's a gift to receive it empathically, connecting with what's alive in them, making no judgment. It's a gift when we try to hear what is alive in the other person and what they would like. So Nonviolent Communication is just a manifestation of what I understand love to be. In that way it's similar to the Judeo-Christian concepts of "Love your neighbor as yourself" and "Judge not lest you be judged."

It's amazing what happens when we connect with people in this way. This beauty, this power connects us with an energy that I choose to call Beloved Divine Energy—one of the many names for God. So Nonviolent Communication helps me stay connected with that beautiful Divine Energy within myself and to connect with it in others. It's the closest thing to "love" I've ever experienced.

## Conclusion

So in relationships, we want to be ourselves, but we want to do that in a way that is respectful to others as well, even if they're not treating us in a particularly respectful way. We want to connect with them, yet we don't want to get caught up in their way of doing business, so how do we do both? I'm suggesting that we do that by expressing ourselves very assertively. NVC is a very assertive language. We can be very loud and clear about what we feel, what our needs are, what we want from the other person, but we're very assertive without doing two things which turn assertiveness into violence. In NVC we assert ourselves but without criticizing the other. So, we say nothing in the language of NVC that in any way implies that the other person is ever wrong. And by wrong I mean about a thousand different things, inappropriate, selfish, insensitive, in fact any word that classifies or categorizes what the other person is.

In NVC we learn how to be very assertive about saying what's going on in us, and we also have the wonderful art when we speak NVC of very assertively telling people what we would like them to do, but we present this to them as a request and not as a demand. Because at the moment people hear from our lips anything that sounds like a criticism or a demand, or it sounds somehow to them like we don't value their needs equal to our needs—when the other person gets that impression from us, that we are only out to get our way, we lose, because then the other person has less energy to sincerely consider our needs. Most of their energy will go into defensiveness or resistance.

We want to be very assertive when we speak NVC in a way that gives the other person our assertiveness as a gift that reveals nakedly what's going on in us, clearly tells us what we would like from them.

I would say the basic human need, the thing that is the greatest feeling for everybody universally is the joy that we feel when we see we have the power to enrich life. I have never met a person who doesn't enjoy giving to other people, provided that it's done willingly. I believe that happens once a person trusts that I am not there trying to coerce them into doing anything and we can keep an NVC dance going where we both just continue to share what we both feel and need, and I have every hope this is happening. In my relationships I get to test out this rosy philosophy quite a bit.

## An Invitation

What's missing from this transcription is the experience of sharing time and space with Marshall Rosenberg or one of the CNVC certified trainers. The power, warmth, and poignancy of the NVC message are amplified by being at a training in person. The interplay with a live audience adds a dimension to the learning process that is hard to match on paper. If you'd like to see Marshall or another CNVC trainer in person, please visit www.CNVC.org for a schedule of NVC trainings and speaking engagements, and a listing of NVC Trainers and Support People around the world.

For a complete up-to-date listing of all NVC materials—audios, CDs, books, and more—please visit www.CNVC.org. For additional NVC information please visit www.NonviolentCommunication.com.

# The Four-Part Nonviolent Communication Process

Clearly expressing
how **I am**
without blaming
or criticizing

Empathically receiving
how **you are**
without hearing
blame or criticism

## OBSERVATIONS

1. What I observe *(see, hear, remember, imagine, free from my evaluations)* that does or does not contribute to my well-being:

   *"When I (see, hear) . . . "*

1. What you observe *(see, hear, remember, imagine, free from your evaluations)* that does or does not contribute to your well-being:

   *"When you see/hear . . . "*

   *(Sometimes unspoken when offering empathy)*

## FEELINGS

2. How I feel *(emotion or sensation rather than thought)* in relation to what I observe:

   *"I feel . . . "*

2. How you feel *(emotion or sensation rather than thought)* in relation to what you observe:

   *"You feel . . ."*

## NEEDS

3. What I need or value *(rather than a preference, or a specific action)* that causes my feelings:

   *" . . . because I need/value . . . "*

3. What you need or value *(rather than a preference, or a specific action)* that causes your feelings:

   *" . . . because you need/value . . ."*

Clearly requesting that
which would enrich **my**
life without demanding

Empathically receiving that
which would enrich **your** life
without hearing any demand

## REQUESTS

4. The concrete actions I would like taken:

   *"Would you be willing to . . . ?"*

4. The concrete actions you would like taken:

   *"Would you like . . . ?"*

   *(Sometimes unspoken when offering empathy)*

© Marshall B. Rosenberg. For more information about Marshall B. Rosenberg or the Center for Nonviolent Communication, please visit www.CNVC.org.

• 65 •

# Some Basic Feelings We All Have

## Feelings when needs are fulfilled

- Amazed
- Comfortable
- Confident
- Eager
- Energetic
- Fulfilled
- Glad
- Hopeful
- Inspired
- Intrigued
- Joyous
- Moved
- Optimistic
- Proud
- Relieved
- Stimulated
- Surprised
- Thankful
- Touched
- Trustful

## Feelings when needs are not fulfilled

- Angry
- Annoyed
- Concerned
- Confused
- Disappointed
- Discouraged
- Distressed
- Embarrassed
- Frustrated
- Helpless
- Hopeless
- Impatient
- Irritated
- Lonely
- Nervous
- Overwhelmed
- Puzzled
- Reluctant
- Sad
- Uncomfortable

# Some Basic Needs We All Have

## Autonomy
- Choosing dreams/goals/values
- Choosing plans for fulfilling one's dreams, goals, values

## Celebration
- Celebrating the creation of life and dreams fulfilled
- Celebrating losses: loved ones, dreams, etc. (mourning)

## Integrity
- Authenticity • Creativity
- Meaning • Self-worth

## Interdependence
- Acceptance • Appreciation
- Closeness • Community
- Consideration
- Contribution to the enrichment of life
- Emotional Safety • Empathy

## Physical Nurturance
- Air • Food
- Movement, exercise
- Protection from life-threatening forms of life: viruses, bacteria, insects, predatory animals
- Rest • Sexual Expression
- Shelter • Touch • Water

## Play
- Fun • Laughter

## Spiritual Communion
- Beauty • Harmony
- Inspiration • Order • Peace

- Honesty (the empowering honesty that enables us to learn from our limitations)
- Love • Reassurance
- Respect • Support
- Trust • Understanding

**About Nonviolent Communication**

From the bedroom to the boardroom, from the classroom to the war zone, Nonviolent Communication (NVC) is changing lives every day. NVC provides an easy-to-grasp, effective method to get to the root of violence and pain peacefully. By examining the unmet needs behind what we do and say, NVC helps reduce hostility, heal pain, and strengthen professional and personal relationships. NVC is now being taught in corporations, classrooms, prisons, and mediation centers worldwide. And it is affecting cultural shifts as institutions, corporations, and governments integrate NVC consciousness into their organizational structures and their approach to leadership.

Most of us are hungry for skills that can improve the quality of our relationships, to deepen our sense of personal empowerment or simply help us communicate more effectively. Unfortunately, most of us have been educated from birth to compete, judge, demand, and diagnose; to think and communicate in terms of what is "right" and "wrong" with people. At best, the habitual ways we think and speak hinder communication and create misunderstanding or frustration. And still worse, they can cause anger and pain, and may lead to violence. Without wanting to, even people with the best of intentions generate needless conflict.

NVC helps us reach beneath the surface and discover what is alive and vital within us, and how all of our actions are based on human needs that we are seeking to meet. We learn to develop a vocabulary of feelings and needs that helps us more clearly express what is going on in us at any given moment. When we understand and acknowledge our needs, we develop a shared foundation for much more satisfying relationships. Join the thousands of people worldwide who have improved their relationships and their lives with this simple yet revolutionary process.

# About PuddleDancer Press

PuddleDancer Press (PDP) is the premier publisher of Nonviolent Communication™ related works. Its mission is to provide high-quality materials to help people create a world in which all needs are met compassionately. Publishing revenues are used to develop new books, and implement promotion campaigns for NVC and Marshall Rosenberg. By working in partnership with the Center for Nonviolent Communication and NVC trainers, teams, and local supporters, PDP has created a comprehensive promotion effort that has helped bring NVC to thousands of new people each year.

Since 2003 PDP has donated more than 60,000 NVC books to organizations, decision-makers, and individuals in need around the world. This program is supported in part by donations made to CNVC and by partnerships with like-minded organizations around the world. PDP is a core partner of the Help Share NVC Project, giving access to hundreds of valuable tools, resources, and ideas to help NVC trainers and supporters make NVC a household name by creating financially sustainable training practices. Learn more at www.helpsharenvc.com.

**Visit the PDP website at www.NonviolentCommunication.com to find the following resources:**

- **Shop NVC**—Continue your learning. Purchase our NVC titles online safely, affordably, and conveniently. Find everyday discounts on individual titles, multiple-copies, and book packages. Learn more about our authors and read endorsements of NVC from world-renowned communication experts and peacemakers.

- **NVC Quick Connect e-Newsletter**—Sign up today to receive our monthly e-Newsletter, filled with expert articles, upcoming training opportunities with our authors, and exclusive specials on NVC learning materials. Archived e-Newsletters are also available

- **About NVC**—Learn more about these life-changing communication and conflict resolution skills including an overview of the NVC process, key facts about NVC, and more.

- **About Marshall Rosenberg**—Access press materials, biography, and more about this world-renowned peacemaker, educator, bestselling author, and founder of the Center for Nonviolent Communication.

- **Free Resources for Learning NVC**—Find free weekly tips series, NVC article archive, and other great resources to make learning these vital communication skills just a little easier.

For more information, please contact PuddleDancer Press at:

2240 Encinitas Blvd., Ste. D-911 • Encinitas, CA 92024
Phone: 858-759-6963 • Fax: 858-759-6967
Email: email@puddledancer.com • www.NonviolentCommunication.com

The Center for Nonviolent Communication (CNVC) is an international nonprofit peacemaking organization whose vision is a world where everyone's needs are met peacefully. CNVC is devoted to supporting the spread of Nonviolent Communication (NVC) around the world.

Founded in 1984 by Dr. Marshall B. Rosenberg, CNVC has been contributing to a vast social transformation in thinking, speaking and acting—showing people how to connect in ways that inspire compassionate results. NVC is now being taught around the globe in communities, schools, prisons, mediation centers, churches, businesses, professional conferences, and more. More than 200 certified trainers and hundreds more teach NVC to approximately 250,000 people each year in 35 countries.

CNVC believes that NVC training is a crucial step to continue building a compassionate, peaceful society. Your tax-deductible donation will help CNVC continue to provide training in some of the most impoverished, violent corners of the world. It will also support the development and continuation of organized projects aimed at bringing NVC training to high-need geographic regions and populations.

To make a tax-deductible donation or to learn more about the valuable resources described below, visit the CNVC website at www.CNVC.org:

- **Training and Certification**—Find local, national, and international training opportunities, access trainer certification information, connect to local NVC communities, trainers, and more.

- **CNVC Bookstore**—Find mail or phone order information for a complete selection of NVC books, booklets, audio, and video materials at the CNVC website.

- **CNVC Projects**—Seven regional and theme-based projects provide focus and leadership for teaching NVC in a particular application or geographic region.

- **E-Groups and List Servs**—Join one of several moderated, topic-based NVC e-groups and list servs developed to support individual learning and the continued growth of NVC worldwide.

For more information, please contact CNVC at:

 5600-A San Francisco Rd., NE, Albuquerque, NM  87109
Ph: 505-244-4041 • Fax: 505-247-0414
Email: cnvc@CNVC.org • Website: www.CNVC.org

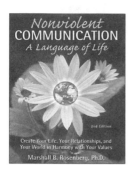

## Nonviolent Communication:
## A Language of Life, Second Edition
*Create Your Life, Your Relationships, and Your World in Harmony With Your Values*

**Marshall B. Rosenberg, Ph.D.**

$19.95 — Trade Paper 6x9, 240pp
ISBN: 978-1-892005-03-8

In this internationally acclaimed text, Marshall Rosenberg offers insightful stories, anecdotes, practical exercises and role-plays that will literally change your approach to communication for the better. Nonviolent Communication partners practical skills with a powerful consciousness to help us get what we want peacefully.

Discover how the language you use can strengthen your relationships, build trust, prevent or resolve conflicts peacefully, and heal pain. More than 400,000 copies of this landmark text have been sold in twenty languages around the globe.

"Nonviolent Communication is a simple yet powerful methodology for communicating in a way that meets both parties' needs. This is one of the most useful books you will ever read."
**—William Ury**, coauthor of *Getting to Yes* and author of *The Third Side*

"I believe the principles and techniques in this book can literally change the world, but more importantly, they can change the quality of your life with your spouse, your children, your neighbors, your co-workers, and everyone else you interact with."
**—Jack Canfield**, author, *Chicken Soup for the Soul*

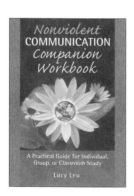

## Nonviolent Communication
## Companion Workbook
*A Practical Guide for Individual, Group, or Classroom Study*

**by Lucy Leu**

$21.95 — Trade Paper 7x10, 224pp
ISBN: 978-1-892005-04-5

Learning Nonviolent Communication has often been equated with learning a whole new language. The *NVC Companion Workbook* helps you put these powerful, effective skills into practice with chapter-by-chapter study of Marshall Rosenberg's cornerstone text, *NVC: A Language of Life*. Create a safe, supportive group learning or practice environment that nurtures the needs of each participant. Find a wealth of activities, exercises, and facilitator suggestions to refine and practice this powerful communication process.

**Available from PuddleDancer Press, the Center for Nonviolent Communication, all major bookstores, and Amazon.com. Distributed by Independent Publisher's Group: 800-888-4741.**

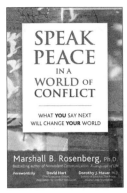

## Speak Peace in a World of Conflict

*What You Say Next Will Change Your World*

**by Marshall B. Rosenberg, Ph.D.**

**$15.95** — Trade Paper 5-3/8x8-3/8, 208pp
ISBN: 978-1-892005-17-5

International peacemaker, mediator, and healer, Marshall Rosenberg shows you how the language you use is the key to enriching life. *Speak Peace* is filled with inspiring stories, lessons, and ideas drawn from more than forty years of mediating conflicts and healing relationships in some of the most war-torn, impoverished, and violent corners of the world. Find insight, practical skills, and powerful tools that will profoundly change your relationships and the course of your life for the better.

Discover how you can create an internal consciousness of peace as the first step toward effective personal, professional, and social change. Find complete chapters on the mechanics of Speaking Peace, conflict resolution, transforming business culture, transforming enemy images, addressing terrorism, transforming authoritarian structures, expressing and receiving gratitude, and social change.

**Bestselling author of the internationally acclaimed,**
*Nonviolent Communication: A Language of Life*

## Being Genuine

*Stop Being Nice, Start Being Real*

**by Thomas d'Ansembourg**

**$17.95** — Trade Paper 5-3/8x8-3/8, 280pp
ISBN: 978-1-892005-21-2

*Being Genuine* brings Thomas d'Ansembourg's blockbuster French title to the English market. His work offers you a fresh new perspective on the proven skills offered in the bestselling book, *Nonviolent Communication: A Language of Life*. Drawing on his own real-life examples and stories, Thomas d'Ansembourg provides practical skills and concrete steps that allow us to safely remove the masks we wear, which prevent the intimacy and satisfaction we desire with our intimate partners, children, parents, friends, family, and colleagues.

"Through this book, we can feel Nonviolent Communication not as a formula but as a rich, meaningful way of life, both intellectually and emotionally."

—**Vicki Robin,** co-founder, Conversation Cafes,
coauthor, *Your Money or Your Life*

**Based on Marshall Rosenberg's Nonviolent Communication process**

Available from PuddleDancer Press, the Center for Nonviolent Communication, all major bookstores, and Amazon.com. Distributed by Independent Publisher's Group: 800-888-4741.

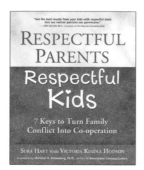

## Respectful Parents, Respectful Kids

*7 Keys to Turn Family Conflict Into Co-operation*

**by Sura Hart and Victoria Kindle Hodson**

**$17.95** — Trade Paper 7.5x9.25, 256pp
ISBN: 978-1-892005-22-9

### Stop the Struggle—Find the Co-operation and Mutual Respect You Want!

Do more than simply correct bad behavior—finally unlock your parenting potential. Use this handbook to move beyond typical discipline techniques and begin creating an environment based on mutual respect, emotional safety, and positive, open communication. *Respectful Parents, Respectful Kids* offers *7 Simple Keys* to discover the mutual respect and nurturing relationships you've been looking for.

### Use these 7 Keys to:

- Set firm limits without using demands or coercion
- Achieve mutual respect without being submissive
- Successfully prevent, reduce, and resolve conflicts
- Empower your kids to open up, co-operate, and realize their full potential
- Make your home a *No-Fault Zone* where trust thrives

## Eat by Choice, Not by Habit

*Practical Skills for Creating a Healthy Relationship With Your Body and Food*

**by Sylvia Haskvitz**

**$10.95** — 5-3/8x8-3/8, 128pp
ISBN: 978-1-892005-20-5

### "Face Your Stuff, or Stuff Your Face"
—anonymous

Eating is a basic human need. But what if you are caught up in the cycles of overconsumption or emotional eating?

Using the consciousness of Nonviolent Communication, *Eat by Choice* helps you dig deeper into the emotional consciousness that underlies your eating patterns. Much more than a prescriptive fad diet, you'll learn practical strategies to develop a healthier relationship with food. Learn to enjoy the tastes, smells, and sensations of healthful eating once again.

**Available from PuddleDancer Press, the Center for Nonviolent Communication, all major bookstores, and Amazon.com. Distributed by Independent Publisher's Group: 800-888-4741.**

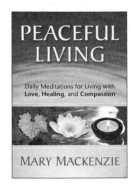

## Peaceful Living

*Daily Meditations for Living With Love,*
*Healing, and Compassion*

**by Mary Mackenzie**

**$19.95** — Trade Paper 5x7.5, 448pp

ISBN: 978-1-892005-19-9

In this gathering of wisdom, Mary Mackenzie empowers you with an intimate life map that will literally change the course of your life for the better. Each of the 366 meditations includes an inspirational quote and concrete, practical tips for integrating the daily message into your life. The learned behaviors of cynicism, resentment, and getting even are replaced with the skills of Nonviolent Communication, including recognizing one's needs and values and making choices in alignment with them.

*Peaceful Living* goes beyond daily affirmations, providing the skills and consciousness you need to transform relationships, heal pain, and discover the life-enriching meaning behind even the most trying situations. Begin each day centered and connected to yourself and your values. Direct the course of your life toward your deepest hopes and needs. Ground yourself in the power of compassionate, conscious living.

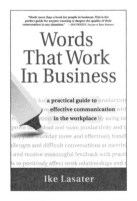

## Words That Work In Business

*A Practical Guide to Effective Communication*
*in the Workplace*

**by Ike Lasater**

**$12.95** — Trade Paper 5-3/8x8-3/8, 144pp

ISBN: 978-1-892005-01-4

### Do You Want to Be Happier, More Effective, and Experience Less Stress at Work?

Do you wish for more respectful work relationships? To move beyond gossip and power struggles, to improved trust and productivity? If you've ever wondered if just one person can positively affect work relationships and company culture, regardless of your position, this book offers a resounding "yes." The key is shifting how we think and talk.

Former attorney-turned-mediator, Ike Lasater, offers practical communication skills matched with recognizable work scenarios to help anyone address the most common workplace relationship challenges. Learn proven communication skills to: Enjoy your workday more; effectively handle difficult conversations; reduce workplace conflict and stress; improve individual and team productivity; be more effective at meetings; and give and receive meaningful feedback.

**Available from PuddleDancer Press, the Center for Nonviolent Communication, all major bookstores, and Amazon.com. Distributed by Independent Publisher's Group: 800-888-4741.**

**Being Me, Loving You:** *A Practical Guide to Extraordinary Relationships* **by Marshall B. Rosenberg, Ph.D.** • Watch your relationships strengthen as you learn to think of love as something you "do," something you give freely from the heart.
80pp, ISBN: 978-1-892005-16-8 • **$8.95**

**Getting Past the Pain Between Us:** *Healing and Reconciliation Without Compromise* **by Marshall B. Rosenberg, Ph.D.** • Learn simple steps to create the heartfelt presence necessary for lasting healing to occur—great for mediators, counselors, families, and couples.
48pp, ISBN: 978-1-892005-07-6 • **$8.95**

**Graduating From Guilt**: *Six Steps to Overcome Guilt and Reclaim Your Life* **by Holly Michelle Eckert** • The burden of guilt leaves us stuck, stressed, and feeling like we can never measure up. Through a proven six-step process, this book helps liberate you from the toxic guilt, blame, and shame you carry.
96pp, ISBN: 978-1-892005-23-6 • **$9.95**

**The Heart of Social Change:** *How to Make a Difference in Your World* **by Marshall B. Rosenberg, Ph.D.** • Learn how creating an internal consciousness of compassion can impact your social change efforts.
48pp, ISBN: 978-1-892005-10-6 • **$8.95**

**Parenting From Your Heart:** *Sharing the Gifts of Compassion, Connection, and Choice* **by Inbal Kashtan** • Filled with insight and practical skills, this booklet will help you transform your parenting to address every day challenges.
48pp, ISBN: 978-1-892005-08-3 • **$8.95**

**Practical Spirituality:** *Reflections on the Spiritual Basis of Nonviolent Communication* **by Marshall B. Rosenberg, Ph.D.** • Marshall's views on the spiritual origins and underpinnings of NVC, and how practicing the process helps him connect to the Divine.
48pp, ISBN: 978-1-892005-14-4 • **$8.95**

**Raising Children Compassionately:** *Parenting the Nonviolent Communication Way* **by Marshall B. Rosenberg, Ph.D.** • Learn to create a mutually respectful, enriching family dynamic filled with heartfelt communication.
32pp, ISBN: 978-1-892005-09-0 • **$7.95**

**The Surprising Purpose of Anger:** *Beyond Anger Management: Finding the Gift* **by Marshall B. Rosenberg, Ph.D.** • Marshall shows you how to use anger to discover what you need, and then how to meet your needs in more constructive, healthy ways.
48pp, ISBN: 978-1-892005-15-1 • **$8.95**

**Teaching Children Compassionately:** *How Students and Teachers Can Succeed With Mutual Understanding* **by Marshall B. Rosenberg, Ph.D.** • In this national keynote address to Montessori educators, Marshall describes his progressive, radical approach to teaching that centers on compassionate connection.
48pp, ISBN: 978-1-892005-11-3 • **$8.95**

**We Can Work It Out:** *Resolving Conflicts Peacefully and Powerfully* **by Marshall B. Rosenberg, Ph.D.** • Practical suggestions for fostering empathic connection, genuine co-operation, and satisfying resolutions in even the most difficult situations.
32pp, ISBN: 978-1-892005-12-0 • **$7.95**

**What's Making You Angry?** *10 Steps to Transforming Anger So Everyone Wins* **by Shari Klein and Neill Gibson** • A powerful, step-by-step approach to transform anger to find healthy, mutually satisfying outcomes.
32pp, ISBN: 978-1-892005-13-7 • **$7.95**

**Available from PuddleDancer Press, the Center for Nonviolent Communication, all major bookstores, and Amazon.com. Distributed by IPG: 800-888-4741. For more information about these booklets or to order online, visit www.NonviolentCommunication.com**

# About the Author

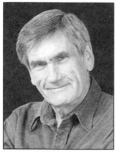

Photo by Beth Banning

**Marshall B. Rosenberg, Ph.D.,** is the founder and director of educational services for the Center for Nonviolent Communication (CNVC), an international peacemaking organization. He is the author of *Speak Peace in a World of Conflict*, and the bestselling *Nonviolent Communication: A Language of Life*. Marshall is the proud recipient of the 2006 Global Village Foundation's Bridge of Peace Award, and the Association of Unity Churches International 2006 Light of God Expressing Award.

Growing up in a turbulent Detroit neighborhood, Marshall developed a keen interest in new forms of communication that would provide peaceful alternatives to the violence he encountered. His interest led to a doctorate in clinical psychology from the University of Wisconsin in 1961, where he studied under Carl Rogers. His subsequent life experience and study of comparative religion motivated him to develop the NVC process.

Marshall first used the NVC process in federally-funded school integration projects during the 1960s to provide mediation and communication skills training. In 1984, he founded CNVC, which is now affiliated with more than 200 certified NVC trainers in 35 countries around the globe.

With guitar and puppets in hand, a history of traveling to some of the most violent corners of the world, and a spiritual energy that fills a room, Marshall shows us how to create a more peaceful and satisfying world. Marshall is currently based in Wasserfallenhof, Switzerland.